A level in a week

Business Studies

Steve Dalton, Abbey Tutorial College
Series editor: Kevin Byrne

Where to find the information you need

Letts Educational
Aldine Place
London W12 8AW
Tel: 0181 740 2266
Fax: 0181 743 8541
e-mail: mail@lettsed.co.uk
website: http://www.lettsed.co.uk

First published 1999

British Library Cataloguing in Publication Data
A CIP record for this book is available from the British Library.

ISBN 185758 9262

Editorial, design and production by Hart McLeod, Cambridge

Printed in Great Britain by Ashford Colour Press

Letts Educational is the trading name of BPP (Letts Educational) Ltd

Contribution and breakeven

15 minutes

Test your knowledge

1. Breakeven occurs where a firm makes neither a profit nor a loss. It is therefore when contribution exactly covers __F__ __C__.

2. Contribution per unit is a key variable. It is defined as __V__ __C__ minus __S__ __P.__ per unit.

3. Profit is any surplus of total revenue over total cost. It is thus contribution per unit multiplied by _____ and then _____ _____ are deducted.

4. When current output exceeds the breakeven output, the firm has a buffer of sales before a loss is made. This buffer is known as the _____ _____ _____.

5. For special (i.e. one-off) order situations, a firm must calculate if there is a positive _____ _____ _____. If there is, the order is potentially profitable.

6. A simplifying assumption of breakeven is that all units of output produced are sold. It therefore neglects the impact of _____ on the decision-making process.

7. In breakeven diagrams, both total revenue and total cost schedules tend to be represented as straight lines. This ignores the possibility of _____ _____ _____ being present on both sales and purchases of materials.

If you got them all right, skip to page 3

Contribution and breakeven

30 minutes

Improve your knowledge

1. **Fixed costs** are incurred even when a firm produces no output. They can only be covered if there is a surplus of the selling price over the variable costs required to make each unit of output.

2. **Contribution per unit** is an important measure because it appears in a variety of breakeven formulae.

   > *remember*
   > *BE =*
   > *FC/Cont pu*

3. **Profit** is what is left after both variable and fixed costs have been deducted from sales revenue. Alternatively it is contribution less fixed costs.

4. The **margin of safety** measures a firm's exposure to reductions in demand for its product. The smaller the margin the greater the risk of failing to cover costs.

5. The firm's normal fixed costs can usually be ignored in **special order** decisions as these are assumed to be met within normal production. However, any extra fixed costs arising out of the special order will have to be taken into account. The total contribution from the special order must more than cover these for the order to be profitable.

6. **Demand** is probably the most important constraint for most firms and therefore it is very unrealistic to assume all output can be sold. Inevitably a firm's stock will tend to fluctuate with movements in the business cycle.

7. Higher levels of **sales** may require the seller to reduce the selling price. Also greater **purchases** of raw material usually lead to a bulk purchasing discount. Such effects would create curves rather than straight lines for **cost** and **revenue**.

✓ *Now learn how to use your knowledge*

Contribution and breakeven

45 minutes

Use your knowledge

Hints

1   A company, Firezone Ltd, manufactures a single product, 'Cracker'. It has prepared the following budget for its production in the forthcoming year:

	£
Direct material per unit of 'Cracker'	15
" labour " " " "	10
Rent on premises per annum	2 000 000
Business rates per annum	500 000
Depreciation of machinery per annum	1 500 000
Insurance of premises per annum	375 000
Selling price per unit of 'Cracker'	60

Current output is 150 000 'Crackers' per annum and there is a full capacity output of 200 000.

(a) State which of the above costs are fixed and which are variable.

(b) Calculate breakeven output per annum.

(c) Calculate the profit made at current and full capacity output.

(d) If Firezone Ltd had a target profit of £2 187 500 at the current level of output, what must the selling price be?

fixed costs are time based
FC/Cont pu

gross profit = TR − TC

use above formula

2 Study the breakeven chart below and answer the following questions.

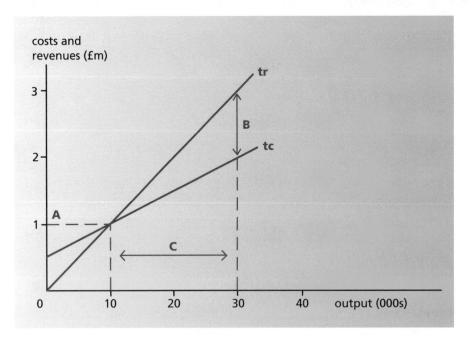

Note – current output is 30 000 units.

(a) What variable is measured at point A?

(b) What is measured by distance B?

(c) What quantity is measured by distance C?

(d) Demonstrate the new breakeven output if the selling price was increased to £125.

not BE output

measured in units

draw a new TR line

Balance sheets and profit and loss accounts

15 minutes

Test your knowledge

1 A balance sheet is a _____ of a firm's financial position at a specific point in time, whilst a profit and loss account is a measure of income over a _____ _____.

2 A balance sheet has to balance the firm's _____ against its _____ and _____.

3 A profit and loss account deducts _____ from _____.

4 An expense which occurs because the cost of a fixed asset has to be spread over its useful life is known as _____.

5 Fixed assets are generally shown in the balance sheet at their _____ _____ _____.

6 Current assets minus current liabilities describe a firm's _____ _____.

7 The portion of the profit and loss account between the turnover and gross profit is known as the _____ _____.

8 A quantity which appears in both the trading account and the balance sheet is _____ _____.

 If you got them all right, skip to page 8

Balance sheets and profit and loss accounts

30 minutes

Improve your knowledge

1 The balance sheet is only applicable for the precise moment in time at which it has been drawn up. Immediately after, transactions may have occurred which change several of the items in the balance sheet. By contrast, the profit and loss account is a historical document which remains a relevant measure of the surplus of revenue over cost for that **time period**.

2 A balance sheet drawn up in horizontal format balances **assets** on the one side against **capital and liabilities** on the other.

3 Profit is the difference between **revenue** and **expenses**.

4 **Depreciation** is an application of the matching concept which states that costs and revenues must be matched together in the same accounting period. As a fixed asset lasts for several years, it would be breaching this concept if the whole cost was treated as an expense in the first year of use.

5 **Net book value** is the remainder of the cost of the fixed asset after deducting all the year's depreciation charges to date. It would, of course, be pure fluke if this value corresponded to the current market value.

6 Current assets minus current liabilities measures the **working capital** of a business, sometimes referred to as 'net current assets'. This is an important measure for a business because it measures the ability to repay debts as they fall due.

7 That part of the profit and loss account which lies between turnover and gross profit is known as the **trading account**. It measures the gross profit, i.e. before overheads are deducted.

8 Certain items appear in both the profit and loss account and the balance sheet. One of these is the **closing stock**. This figure arises out of the end of year stocktake and is used to establish the value of the cost of sales for the year, but is also a current asset.

Now learn how to use your knowledge

Balance sheets and profit and loss accounts

45 minutes

Use your knowledge

Hints

1 The following data refers to Tacky plc for the year ended 30 June 1998.

	£
Loan	150 000
Stock	25 000
Ordinary share capital	200 000
Debtors	75 000
Bank	50 000
Cash	5 000
Revaluation reserve	40 000
Tax	15 000
Retained profit	95 000
Trade creditors	25 000
Proposed dividends	25 000
Land	175 000
Buildings	100 000
Vehicles	50 000
Fixtures	70 000

(a) Draw up a horizontal balance sheet as at 30 June 1998.

$A = L + C$

During 1 July 1998 the following transactions took place:

1 the dividends were paid by cheque
2 £20 000 of the loan was paid by cheque
3 shareholders purchased £50 000 more share capital in the firm and paid by cheque
4 the land was revalued at £200 000
5 new vehicles were bought for £10 000 by cheque.

(b) Draw up a balance sheet in vertical format as at 1 July 1998.

(c) Calculate working capital and explain why this is an important quantity for a business.

(d) Explain what is meant by a 'revaluation reserve'.

(e) Why are most fixed assets depreciated each year in the accounts?

(f) Why is land often not depreciated?

(g) State three reasons why a balance sheet may not be an accurate valuation of the business at that date.

(h) Why does retained profit appear on the balance sheet?

Hints

land and buildings

freehold

who does it belong to?

Answers on page 60

Ratio analysis

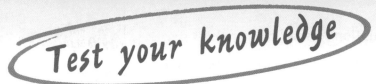

Test your knowledge

15 minutes

1 The key to the usefulness of ratio analysis is the ability to be able to make _____.

2 The main two types of the above are:

(a) With the same company results from _____ periods.

(b) With a similar company in the same _____ _____.

3 The gearing ratio measures a company's _____ _____.

4 Ratios such as debtors' or stock turnover measure how efficiently a company uses its _____.

5 The ROCE ratio should be significantly larger than the return from money invested in, e.g. a building society because of the extra _____ involved.

6 Liquidity ratios measure a company's ability to avoid _____.

7 A constant gross profit ratio combined with a declining net profit ratio means the company is having problems controlling its _____.

8 A high gearing ratio for a company is seen as implying that it presents a _____ investment for the ordinary shareholder.

Ratio analysis

Improve your knowledge

30 minutes

1   Ratios can only reveal a limited amount of information about a company if they are analysed in isolation. A much greater depth of understanding is possible if certain **comparisons** can be made. These enable trends to be uncovered and relative measures of efficiency to be employed.

2   (a) Trends over time can be detected by making a comparison with the same company's results in a previous **period**.

       (b) Relative measures of efficiency can be deduced from using a comparison with another company in the same **business sector**. Often this is difficult in practice because even companies in the same industry can differ in their size, capital structure etc.

3   Gearing is a measure of a company's **capital structure**. It measures the proportion of total capital that has been obtained from debt or loan sources rather than from equity sources. The higher the gearing of a company the greater the level of risk due to the enhanced exposure to changes in interest rates. Also highly geared companies may experience problems in raising new finance.

4   Collectively known as activity ratios, these measure the degree of efficient **asset** utilisation. Debtor and stock turnover needs to be brisk in order to avoid cash flow problems.

5   Leaving money in a building society is an example of a **risk** free asset which will tend to have a relatively low return. The **ROCE** ratio for a manufacturing company, for example, carries much higher risk and therefore capital providers will expect a correspondingly higher return.

6   Liquidity ratios measure the likelihood of a company falling into **insolvency**, i.e. being unable to pay its debts as they fall due. The acid test ratio is particularly useful as it excludes stock which is the least liquid of current assets and is thus not ideally suited to paying debts.

7 The two ratios can be used together to assess the ability of the company to control their **overheads**.

8 High gearing is seen as **risky** as its profits are likely to fluctuate to a greater extent than a company with low gearing.

Ratio analysis

Use your knowledge

1 Texco Ltd has produced the following balance sheet for the year ended 31 December 1998.

	£	£
Fixed assets		
Buildings		500 000
Machinery		275 000
		775 000
Current assets		
Stock	75 000	
Debtors	190 000	
Cash at bank	20 000	
	285 000	
Current liabilities		
Creditors	(185 000)	
Net current assets		100 000
		875 000
Long term liabilities		
Loan		(150 000)
		725 000
Capital and reserves		
Ordinary share capital (£1 shares)		400 000
Share premium		50 000
Revaluation reserve		75 000
Retained profit		200 000
		725 000

For the year ended 31 December 1998 the following information is available for Texco Ltd:

Net profit	£95 000
Interest paid	£18 000
Turnover	£975 000
Cost of sales	£425 000

(a) Calculate ROCE and comment on its value.

(b) Calculate two liquidity ratios and comment on their value.

(c) Calculate debtors' and stock turnover and explain what they have measured.

measured in days

(d) Calculate gearing and interpret its magnitude.

borderline 50/50

(e) State three consequences of a company having a high gearing ratio.

think risk

(f) Explain two ways in which a company can reduce its gearing.

(g) State four features of a company's performance which are not revealed by financial ratios.

i.e. qualitative

(h) Suggest two ways a company could improve its acid test ratio.

Answers on page 62

Cash flow management

15 minutes

Test your knowledge

1 'Cash' refers to cash in notes and coins and also cash _____ _____.

2 Cash is the most _____ of all assets and thus has unique uses.

3 Good cash flow management can be seen as striking an acceptable balance between _____ and _____.

4 Cash flow involves time lags. A business wants the debtor's paying time lag to be _____ and the creditor's paying time lag to be _____.

5 If there are breaks in the cash flow cycle, the business may be unable to pay its _____ as they fall due and may thus face bankruptcy.

6 One way to improve cash flow is, rather than purchasing fixed assets, to _____ them instead.

7 Another is to establish proper credit control procedures, such as setting each customer a definite _____ _____.

8 Such procedures are not necessary if the business outsources its debt collection procedures, i.e. by appointing a _____ _____.

9 There is a very important difference between the net cash inflow for a business in a year and its reported _____ _____ for the same year.

Answers

 If you got them all right, skip to page 18

15

Cash flow management

Improve your knowledge

1 'Cash' is a wider term than just notes and coins – it also includes **cash at bank**. There is little to choose between these two with regard to liquidity.

2 Cash is the most **liquid** of all assets and it is therefore uniquely placed to function as a universally acceptable means of exchange and, in particular, as the medium used to accept payments in settlement of debts.

3 **Liquidity and profitability** are two conflicting aims of financial management. The former is vital to keep the business safe from insolvency, whilst the latter is necessary to attract capital providers to lend funds to the business.

4 Some time lags are beneficial to a business whilst others are a hindrance. It is of benefit for the debtor's paying period to be **short** whilst the creditor's paying period is of benefit when **long**.

5 Cash needs to be regularly and smoothly running through a business, often shown as a **cash flow cycle**. If there is an interruption to this flow, for example caused by a rash of bad **debts**, the survival of the business may be at risk as debts may not be paid as they fall due.

6 Major purchases of fixed assets, especially at the inchoate stage of a business, can act as a substantial drain on cash. Many businesses therefore prefer to **lease** them instead. Leasing illustrates the conflict between the objectives of liquidity and profitability as it eases the strain on cash flow, but probably works out more expensive in the long term.

7 The adoption of appropriate credit control procedures helps to minimise the risk of suffering large scale bad debts. One part of this is to set each customer a **credit limit** based on perceived risk, size, references etc.

8 An increasing trend in modern business is for firms to employ the services of an external **debt factor**. The debt factor then shoulders much of the burden of the credit sales administration.

9 A variety of reasons causes there to be an often substantial difference between net cash inflow for a period and reported **profit** for the same period.

✔ *Now learn how to use your knowledge*

Cash flow management

Use your knowledge

1 A company is in its first year of operation and has 150 000 £1 shares and a £25 000 bank loan at 15% interest.

In its first year it paid for the following items:

	£
Machinery	100 000
Raw materials	175 000
Wages	80 000
Overheads	30 000

Tax is 25% of net profit but, like the £15 000 dividends proposed, does not have to be paid until the second year.

Depreciation of machinery is a straight line, over ten years, with a zero scrap value.

During the year 1000 units of product were sold at £250 each, but 100 had not been paid for by year end.

Closing stock was £75 000.

(a) Calculate the cash balance at the end of the year.

(b) Calculate the profit carried forward to next year.

only cash movements

fair measure

2 Give three reasons why any firm's net cash inflow for a year may differ from its profit for the year.

3 Give two reasons why a business would prepare a cash flow forecast.

not legally required

4 Explain two actions a firm could take to solve an immediate cash crisis.

5 If the company above was said to be 'overtrading', what would this mean?

6 Which of the possible company stakeholders is most concerned about liquidity as opposed to profitability? Explain your answer.

Answers on page 64

Investment appraisal

15 minutes

Test your knowledge

1 Investment appraisal is concerned with evaluating _____ expenditure projects.

2 Payback and net present value methods evaluate _____ _____, whilst average rate of return evaluates _____.

3 Net present value method uses _____ _____ _____ in order to convert future cash flows into their present value.

4 Due to the long time horizons involved, capital projects carry a high degree of _____.

5 Financial aspects are not the only factors to take into account with capital projects; _____ _____ are important too.

6 In net present value method, the cost of capital is used as the _____ _____ in the calculations.

7 Businesses only proceed with capital investment projects when they feel _____ about the future.

8 All methods of investment appraisal use _____ data and are therefore potentially unreliable.

9 A net present value of zero for a project means that the rate of return on the project is equal to the _____ _____.

Investment appraisal

Improve your knowledge

1 **Capital** expenditure is that used to purchase fixed assets which have an expected life of several years. It is usually decided at top management level because of the large sums involved and the long time horizon.

2 Both the payback and net present value methods of investment appraisal share in common an evaluation of **cash flows**, whilst the average rate of return method concentrates on **profits**. Cash flows are seen as less ambiguous than profits as the latter depend on which accounting policies are used.

3 The net present value method uses **discounted cash flow**, a technique which seeks to quote all future receipts/payments of cash in present value terms. This enables receipts and payments from different periods to be compared in the same time zone. As a consequence of the time value of money, cash received now is worth more than cash received in the future. This is because such cash could be invested at the current rate of interest if received now rather than in the future.

4 Capital projects involve a high degree of **risk** as a very long time horizon is usually involved. The longer the time horizon, the greater the uncertainty and therefore the likelihood of events failing to match the estimates. This is one reason why there is still considerable support for the payback technique of investment appraisal. As it concentrates on the short term, it is more likely to recommend a low risk project, at least with regard to the time factor.

5 The three methods under consideration here focus exclusively on the financial aspects and do not take a variety of **qualitative** considerations into account. Qualitative factors are non-financial in nature and can cover a diversity of issues.

6 The net present value method requires a **discount rate** to reduce future cash receipts back to their present values. The rate is supposed to reflect the opportunity cost of using funds in the project rather than elsewhere and is referred to as the cost of capital.

7 As long-term commitments of funds involves the taking of a substantial risk, businesses are only willing to do this when they feel **confident** about both their own prospects and those of the economy as a whole. This explains why, after a recession, investment takes a long time to recover. Business confidence is quite fragile and once dented takes a great deal of rebuilding.

8 Something that all the three methods of investment appraisal share in common is that they use **estimated** data. Such data is inherently unreliable and is unlikely to be realised in practice.

9 Where, by fluke, a project turns out to have a net present value of zero, it means that the expected rate of return on the project is equal to the **discount rate**.

Now learn how to use your knowledge

Investment appraisal

Use your knowledge

Hints

1 A company is considering investing in two projects: Ash and Rowan. Both cost £50 000 and have annual operating costs of £2000. Expected annual cash inflows from sales are:

	Ash £	Rowan £
Year 1	10 000	10 000
" 2	10 000	20 000
" 3	10 000	20 000
" 4	20 000	13 500
" 5	30 000	3 500
" 6	30 000	–
" 7	30 000	–

The market rate of interest is 10%.

(a) Calculate the payback period of the two projects.

(b) Calculate the average rate of return of the two projects.

(c) Calculate the discount factors for years 0 to 7 at a 10% discount rate.

(d) Calculate the net present value of the two projects.

(e) Explain which project is more attractive on financial grounds.

(f) State two advantages and two disadvantages of the payback method of investment appraisal.

(g) What is the advantage of using methods which involve the discounting process?

(h) State four non-financial factors a firm should take into account when planning capital expenditure.

need to cover cost

$\dfrac{1}{(1+r)^n}$

time value of money

Answers on page 65

23

Targeting the market

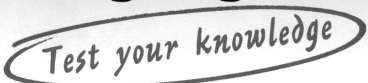

15 minutes

1 A marketing strategy which consists of aiming one product at the whole market is known as _____ _____.

2 A marketing strategy which consists of aiming different products at different segments of the market is known as _____ _____.

3 _____ _____ is a third alternative which concentrates efforts on one small segment of the market.

4 One approach to segmenting a market is to divide consumers into groups A, B, C1 etc., i.e. by their _____ _____.

5 A more modern and sophisticated method that is increasingly popular is to segment a market by consumer _____, i.e. their habits and activities.

6 Another approach based upon demographic patterns is to use _____ to segment a market.

7 Different segments of a market require the use of contrasting styles of advertising, placed in quite different _____ _____.

8 Failure to target promotions at the correct segmented audience results in a high degree of advertising _____ which is unproductive expenditure for a firm.

24

Targeting the market

Improve your knowledge

1. **Undifferentiated marketing** is sometimes described as mass marketing. The market is seen as so homogeneous that segmenting is either impossible or not worthwhile.

2. **Differentiated marketing** is used when the market can easily be divided up into clearly defined segments based on one of a variety of characteristics.

3. **Niche marketing** is where attention is concentrated on one very small part of a market, where there is perceived to be a gap. A firm entering a niche market can therefore enjoy a temporary absence of competition.

4. This places consumers into a **social class** grouping based on occupation. For example, skilled manual workers are categorised as C2.

5. **Lifestyle** is a richer concept than social class and encompasses, for example, attitudes, place of residence and choice of leisure activities.

6. **Age** is an important divider as tastes and inclinations vary very considerably with it. Also with constantly changing demographic patterns, it is important for firms to be aware of the impact this will have on the market for their products.

7. Television and newspapers are examples of **advertising media**, but there are also crucially important differences *within* different elements of the same media. For example, between which programmes should an advertisement best be placed to reach a C1 audience?

8. **Wastage** occurs when an advertisement fails to reach the designated target audience and instead reaches a different one.

Now learn how to use your knowledge

25

Targeting the market

45 minutes

Use your knowledge

Hints

1 Define the concept 'market segment'.

2 Give six characteristics which can be used to segment a market.

3 Explain the benefits to a firm of making use of market segmentation.

think about its appeal

4 Give two advantages and two disadvantages of using a niche marketing strategy.

what are the risks?

5 The Good Times Ltd holiday company is undergoing a fundamental review of its service portfolio and wishes to make full use of market segmentation in order to tailor its holidays to the various consumer requirements. Explain how the characteristics of:

(a) age
(b) lifestyle
(c) social class

horses for courses

may be used to divide the holiday market into specifically identifiable market segments.

Answers on page 67

Pricing strategies

15 minutes

1 When deciding on an appropriate pricing strategy, a business must decide what the main objective is to be. For example, is it to _____ _____ in the short term or is it to build up its _____ _____ in the long term?

2 In very competitive markets, businesses may have very little influence over the price they can charge for their product. Such firms are therefore _____ _____.

3 For firms that are able to influence their price a variety of different pricing policies could be adopted:

(a) _____ _____ uses a low initial price to gain a foothold in the market and establish market share.

(b) The opposite approach of _____ _____ uses a high price to maximise profits whilst the product is at an early stage of its life cycle.

(c) A policy of _____ _____ identifies those segments of the market where demand is strongest and charges a premium price to those segments.

(d) An approach favoured by accountants is to use _____ _____ pricing which identifies the full unit cost to make a product and then adds a mark-up for profit.

(e) _____ _____ uses a price below a product's cost of production in order to eliminate the competition from a market.

4 Whenever a business wishes to alter the price of a product it needs to consider the _____ _____ of _____. A value of less than one means a product with _____ _____. A value of more than one means a product with _____ _____.

If you got them all right, skip to page 29

Pricing strategies

Improve your knowledge

30 minutes

1. Where a firm wishes to **maximise profits** this implies a strategy which uses premium pricing, such as market skimming or price discrimination. Where a build up of **market share** is sought a policy such as penetration pricing, which undercuts the competitors, would be employed.

2. Firms are **price takers** where the market is so competitive that any excess charged over the market price leads to the complete loss of customers.

3. (a) **Penetration pricing** prices low to maximise sales.
   (b) **Market skimming** prices high to maximise profit.
   (c) **Price discrimination** splits customers into clearly defined groups in order to charge the maximum each group is able and willing to pay.
   (d) **Cost based** pricing uses the absorption costing method of allocating overheads to products and then a suitable mark-up is added to obtain the final selling price. A drawback with this approach is that it is less market orientated than other methods.
   (e) **Predatory pricing** identifies weaker rivals and charges a low price on a temporary basis with the aim of driving the rival out of the market, after which prices would be increased again.

4. **Price elasticity of demand** measures the responsiveness of the demand for a product to changes in its price. The formula uses percentage changes:

   $$PED = \frac{\% \text{ change in quantity demanded}}{\% \text{ change in price}}$$

   A value of less than one means that the percentage change in demand is less than the percentage change in price. Such a product is said to have **inelastic demand**.

   A value greater than one means that the percentage change demand outweighs the percentage change in price. This product would be said to have **elastic demand**.

✓ *Now learn how to use your knowledge*

28

Pricing strategies

Use your knowledge

Hints

1 Give two reasons why a product may have inelastic demand with respect to price.

cigarettes

2 A firm believes that its product has a PED of minus two. It is considering increasing the price from £20 to £25. The current level of sales is 500 units per week. State whether, and by how much, total revenue will change.

use PED formula

3 A firm makes three products, Tom, Jerry and Spike. It calculates its prices using the cost based pricing method.

	Tom £	Jerry £	Spike £
Direct costs (per unit)	100	50	200
Total sales in units	2000	5000	3000

Total overheads are £800 000 and these are to be split between the products on the basis of the level of sales of each product.

A mark-up on cost of 25% is to be added.

Calculate the selling price of each product.

allocate overheads in proportion to sales units

4 Why might it be unfair to split overheads on the basis of sales units?

Answers on page 68

Lean production and stock control

15 minutes

Test your knowledge

1 The essence of Japanese lean production methods is for _____ _____ to be kept to the absolute minimum.

2 Instead of having a target of, e.g. 3% failure rate in quality control, lean producers aim for _____ _____.

3 An approach to quality which encourages workers to see the recipient of their output as a 'customer', even when they are fellow employees, is known as _____ _____ _____.

4 _____-_____-_____ is the application of lean production philosophy to stock control systems.

5 The contrasting, traditional approach to stock control is to hold some _____ _____ as a safeguard against fluctuations in demand or supplier unreliability.

6 The level of stock at which a new request for a delivery takes place is known as the _____ _____.

7 If average usage of raw materials is 20 kg per week, buffer stock is 50 kg and the reorder level is 110 kg, calculate the lead time in weeks.

8 Absolute certainty of demand coupled with perfect reliability of suppliers may allow a manufacturer to hold a buffer stock of _____.

Answers

1 resource use   **2** zero defects   **3** total quality management
4 just-in-time   **5** buffer stock   **6** reorder level   **7** three weeks
8 zero

 If you got them all right, skip to page 33

30

Lean production and stock control

Improve your knowledge

1 Traditional mass production systems were seen as using an excessive quantity of inputs. Lean production seeks to keep **resource use** to the absolute minimum by reducing waste as much as possible.

2 **Zero defects** requires a quality target that has been realistically set, based upon an impeccable design and produced by very accurate and dependable production systems. It literally means perfect quality every time.

3 **Total quality management** depends on the creation of a 'culture of quality' which is supported by all management and employees. All functions within a firm are recast into relationships between an invented 'customer' and 'supplier'.

4 The **just-in-time** system minimises the various costs of holding stock by effectively abolishing the idea of a buffer or safety stock. This is consistent with the lean production philosophy of minimising waste. Space formerly used to store stock is now released for alternative purposes such as production.

5 **Buffer stock** is held as a hedge against sudden surges in customer demand or the failure of supplies to arrive at the expected time. More buffer stock is needed in uncertain situations, but this increases stock holding costs.

6 The **reorder level** is the level to which stock must fall in order to trigger a new requisition for supplies. In computerised stock control systems that use the EPOS principle, this reordering takes place automatically.

7 Buffer stock + **lead time** usage = reorder level
   50 kg   +   20 kg × **3**   =   110 kg

8 As buffer stock is held as a hedge against a variety of uncertainties, a perfectly predictable environment would remove the need for it. Thus the safety stock could be **zero** and this is the ideal situation to use just-in-time.

✓ *Now learn how to use your knowledge*

Lean production and stock control

45 minutes

Use your knowledge

Hints

think waste

opportunity cost

think about information

1. State four key aspects of the lean production ethos.

2. State three costs of holding large quantities of stock.

3. Explain two advantages and two disadvantages of a firm changing to a computerised stock control (EPOS) system.

4. The diagram below shows a traditional stock control chart:

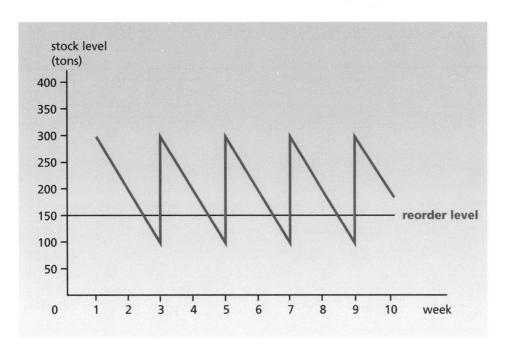

(a) What is the average stock usage per week?

(b) What is the level of buffer stock held?

(c) How long is the lead time in weeks?

(d) What is the size of each fortnightly delivery?

(e) What would be the level of buffer stock if stock usage increased to 150 tons per week and the lead time became one week?

slope becomes steeper

 A manufacturer uses 10 000 kg each year of a raw material AXMA, in the production of its products. The current price of AXMA is £5 per kilo. The lead time is two weeks, the order quantity is 2500 kg and buffer stock is 2000 kg. Assuming a 50 week year, calculate:

(a) reorder level

(b) the number of deliveries required each year

(c) assuming the average quantity of stock held during the year is 3250 kg and a rate of interest of 6% per annum, calculate the annual opportunity cost of holding stock.

average usage during lead time + buffer stock = reorder level

Answers on page 69

Network analysis

Test your knowledge

1 Critical path or network analysis is a technique used to plan and control a wide variety of _____.

2 Two key elements of the process are to determine the _____ _____ through the network and to establish the overall project _____.

3

A | B

In the key opposite, A measures the earliest possible time an activity can commence, known as the _____ _____ _____.

B measures the latest possible time an activity can end without increasing the project duration, known as the _____ _____ _____.

4 Some activities drawn on networks are not real jobs at all and are drawn merely to indicate the correct sequence tasks. These tasks are known as _____.

5 Where an activity can be delayed without lengthening the overall project duration, it is said to have _____.

6 Activities on the critical path have no such _____ and any delays to these jobs will lengthen the overall project duration.

7 When determining ESTs, from left to right, the _____ value is taken when there is a choice.

8 When determining LFTs, from right to left, the _____ value is taken when there is a choice.

Answers

1 projects 2 critical path, duration 3 earliest start time, latest finish time 4 dummies 5 float 6 slack 7 longest 8 shortest

 If you got them all right, skip to page 38

Network analysis

Improve your knowledge

1 Construction **projects**, e.g. a new runway for an airport, would be likely to use critical path analysis. It clarifies the precise ordering of tasks and highlights those which must be completed on time in order to meet the completion deadline.

2 The **critical path** is the longest route through the network and shows a chain of activities which must be finished at their designated time. The project **duration** would normally be used to set a deadline date for project completion. Failure to adhere to this deadline may lead to a penalty charge for the contractor.

3 **Earliest start time** is found by adding the preceding EST to the preceding activity duration. Where there is a choice of times the longest is taken.

Latest finish time is found by subtracting the succeeding activity durations from the succeeding LFT. Where there is a choice, the shortest is taken.

4 A **dummy** activity has a zero duration and flows from the event after the shorter job to the event after the longer job. The subsequent activity starts from where the dummy activity ends.

5 **Float** is spare time or slack, which enables an activity to be delayed without adding to the overall project duration (total float) or next activity (free float).

6 By definition, jobs on the **critical path** have no float or **slack** as they cannot be delayed without adding to the project duration.

7 Where an event has two or more activities approaching it, the **longest** of the respective ESTs is taken. This is because the next dependent activity cannot be started until all the preceding activities for that event are finished.

8 Where an event has two or more activities starting from it, the **shortest** of the possible LFTs is taken. This applies when working backwards through the network, from right to left.

Network analysis

Use your knowledge

Hints

1   Pogo plc is in the process of launching a new product and has drawn up a series of required time activities and the relationships between them.

Job	Preceding job	Weeks
A	–	5
B	A	6
C	A	2
D	B and C	3
E	–	3
F	E	8
G	D	4
H	G	2
I	H and F	10
J	H and F	7
K	H and F	9
L	I and K	3

(a) Draw the network and state the minimum number of weeks the launch can be completed in.

(b) State the critical path for the project.

(c) Calculate the total float for all the activities.

(d) Due to labour supply problems, Pogo plc is trying to identify two jobs which can have staff withdrawn from them but will not result in delay to the whole project. Identify two such jobs and state precisely how long they can be delayed before they lengthen the whole project.

(e) How can network analysis be used to maximise the benefits of just-in-time?

final EST

longest path through network

✓ *Answers on page 71*

Human resource management

15 minutes

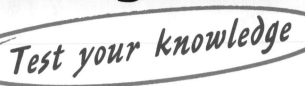

Test your knowledge

1 Human resource management sees _____ as a key resource in modern business organisations.

2 The aim of HRM is to manage and develop their personnel in order to maximise the chances of achieving the firm's _____ _____.

3 An important emphasis of HRM is the need for organisations to encourage their employees continuously to invest in and develop their _____ _____.

4 Such investment in workers' capabilities is achieved through regular _____ programmes at frequent intervals to ensure workplace skills keep pace with technological change.

5 Training can often suffer from under-investment by firms because of the dangers of their staff, once better trained, being _____ by a rival company.

6 A high degree of _____ _____ is seen as a threat to the achievement of HRM goals because of its disruptive effects and the costs of regularly re-advertising posts.

7 HRM recognises the need to be aware of potentially far reaching _____ _____ which mean that employers in the future may face a work-force with a significantly different age structure.

8 One way of regularly assessing the performance of staff is to engage in an annual _____ system.

Answers

1 people 2 corporate objectives 3 human capital 4 training 5 poached 6 labour turnover 7 demographic changes 8 appraisal

If you got them all right, skip to page 42

Human resource management

30 minutes

Improve your knowledge

1. Human resource management is a spin-off from the various Japanese initiatives in managing people. Similar to the personnel function, it has a distinct emphasis on seeing **people** as one of many resources within a business, but having specific needs of its own. The aim is to manage human resources so that the firm can extract the maximum benefit from their deployment.

2. A firm's **corporate objectives** are the overall aims of the business and they are unlikely to be realised without the most productive deployment of a firm's human resources.

3. The productivity of any work-force is partly a function of the level of investment in its **human capital**. Not only should this increase a firm's productivity and effectiveness, it should also enhance the individual worker's earning power. Part of the remuneration of a highly skilled employee could be regarded as a return on the investment in that person's human capital.

4. Investment in human capital can be through either an education or **training** programme. On-the-job training enhances work-based skills and takes place at the usual workplace. Off-the-job training may be wider in scope and take place at a company national training centre.

5. Training carries a high degree of externalities in that, if provided for an employee by an employer, it can potentially benefit other rival firms. As most skills are portable with the employee, a competitor may, at some future stage, **poach** trained staff and thus benefit from the training provision as a free rider. This problem creates an inbuilt bias against an adequate national expenditure on training.

6 Firms which experience a high degree of **labour turnover** encounter a variety of problems. The regularity of staffing changes causes a major disruption to the organisation's business. Additionally, there are several wasteful expenses incurred, such as the costs of frequently retraining new staff and re-advertising vacant positions.

7 The 'demographic time bomb' describes the fact that the age structure of the work-force is likely to change significantly. **Demographic changes** mean that there will be fewer young people as a proportion of the work-force.

8 The annual **appraisal** interview is an opportunity for managers to review the effectiveness of each individual employee. Perhaps rather in conflict, annual appraisal interviews are seen as an opportunity to assess performance, possibly linked to the size of a pay award, to identify training needs and assist employees to reach their full potential.

Now learn how to use your knowledge

Human resource management

Use your knowledge

Hints

1 What is meant by the term 'empowerment'?

think power

2 What measures are taken to offset the inbuilt bias towards inadequate training?

3 State the formula used to measure the labour turnover in a firm.

turnover means leaving

4 What are the possible causes of high labour turnover in a business?

Herzberg?

5 What are the various drawbacks of high labour turnover for a company?

6 Describe the various ways a UK manufacturing company may alleviate the damaging effects of the 'demographic time bomb'.

7 What is the 'core and periphery' model of the labour market?

full-time/casual

8 Assess the advantages and disadvantages of a firm having a 'flexible' work-force.

Answers on page 72

Work and remuneration

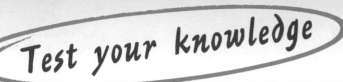

Test your knowledge

1 The management theorist _____ _____ believed money to be the sole reason why employees turned up for work.

2 Pay systems founded upon such principles therefore attempt to find a way of linking an employee's pay to _____ of work undertaken.

3 A problem, however, with such 'piecework' type systems, is that in many service sector occupations, it is not easy to find a quantifiable measure of _____.

4 Modern remuneration systems based on these principles are therefore more sophisticated in their measurement of an employee's contribution to the attainment of the business's objectives. Such systems are described as _____ _____ _____.

5 A key aspect of the contemporary pay scene is the government's introduction of a _____ _____ _____ of £3.60 per hour for adult employees.

6 Much of the controversy surrounding the introduction of this idea revolved around its possible impact on the UK level of _____.

7 By contrast there was also debate about whether there would be a positive impact on the level of employee _____.

8 The management theorist _____ _____ believed that whilst low pay was a serious demotivator, high pay did not necessarily have a positive effect.

Answers

1 Frederick Taylor   2 quantity   3 output
4 performance related pay   5 national minimum wage
6 unemployment   7 motivation   8 Frederick Herzberg

 If you got them all right, skip to page 46

Work and remuneration

Improve your knowledge

30 minutes

1. **Frederick Taylor** created the scientific management school of thought with its associated work study methods. He believed the route to efficiency was a combination of piece-rate payment systems and tight management control.

2. Piece-rate payment systems seek to relate the financial rewards for an employee to the **quantity** of work.

3. Such systems are notoriously difficult to apply in the service sector due to the problem of identifying a suitable measure of **output**. In this sector, output is often of the 'invisible' kind and is qualitative rather than quantitative in nature.

4. **Performance related pay** is a modern variant which seeks to reintroduce the financial calculus into an employee's motivation. It is usually awarded as a bonus or salary increase above norm, following an appraisal interview.

5. The trade union movement has long campaigned for a **national minimum wage** to bring the UK into line with other advanced countries. However, they were disappointed at the relatively low level of the rate set.

6 Much of the opposition to the principle of a minimum wage is related to its alleged impact on the level of **unemployment**. In the diagram below:

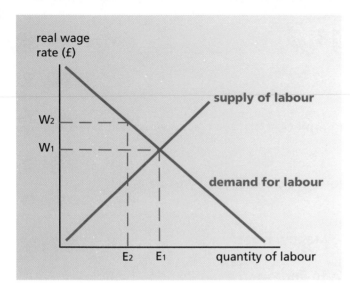

an increase in the wage rate from W1 to W2 reduces the employer's demand for workers from E1 to E2.

In this way, a minimum wage is said to 'price low paid workers out of their jobs'.

However, the reality of the labour market is much more complex than this and the outcome depends on how other factors change in relation to the higher wage rate. For example, levels of training and productivity effects could enhance the demand for labour.

7 A higher hourly pay rate may create a greater feeling of employee **motivation** in the job. However, whether the employee gains financially depends on the degree to which they receive income related benefits such as housing benefit or family credit.

8 **Frederick Herzberg** believed that higher pay, whilst reducing the demotivating effects of low pay, failed to motivate an employee positively.

Now learn how to use your knowledge

Work and remuneration

45 minutes

Use your knowledge

Hints

think quality

1 Give two disadvantages of using a piece-work payment system on a manufacturing production line.

2 Name two other theorists who did not believe money to be an effective motivator at work.

3 What were the five levels of the Maslow hierarchy?

4 Explain three non-financial ways to improve the motivation of employees.

5 Taylor favoured a fairly rigid 'division of labour'. Explain the meaning of this and outline its drawbacks.

6 What was the 'Hawthorne Effect' and what school of management did it create?

7 Why do many managers, particularly in small firms, continue to ignore 'Hawthorne' type ideas in their own workplaces?

8 Assess the case for and against introducing a system of performance related pay for nurses at an elderly persons' care home.

nursing is a profession

9 Consider the possible employer reactions to the introduction of the national minimum wage.

Answers on page 73

Decision trees

Test your knowledge

1 Decision trees allow a _____ approach to be applied to the decision making process.

2 In decision tree diagrams, squares represent _____ points and circles represent _____ points.

3 Whenever a circle appears with more than one possible result, _____ have to be used to value the overall outcome.

4

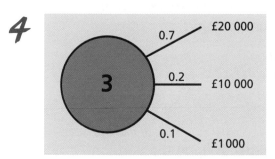

Calculate the value at outcome point 3.

5 Whenever a square appears, the value is obtained by taking the _____ of the various decision values.

6 Decisions are characterised by choosing the options which create the greatest _____ _____.

7 A square denotes a situation where _____ exist and a management decision has to be made.

8 One disadvantage of making decisions on the basis of expected values is that they do not take _____ into account.

Answers

1 quantitative 2 decision, outcome 3 probabilities 4 £16 100
5 highest 6 expected values 7 choices 8 risk

If you got them all right, skip to page 49

47

Decision trees

Improve your knowledge

30 minutes

1 **Quantitative** approaches to decision making are generally seen as preferable to those which rely on a personal hunch. It is possible to gain a clear pictorial account of the alternatives available and the possible outcomes. However, both the probabilities and the valued outcomes are only estimates and both are subject to error.

2 The convention is for a **decision** to be shown as a square and an **outcome** to be shown as a circle.

3 **Probabilities** are used to value the possible results at an outcome point. The probabilities at any outcome point must sum to unity.

4 The value at outcome point 3 = $\quad$ 0.7 × £20 000
$$+ 0.2 \times £10\,000$$
$$+ 0.1 \times \quad £1\,000$$
$$= £16\,100$$

5 The meaning of the '**highest**' expected value depends upon the decision objective. If the objective is to maximise contribution, the largest value would be chosen. However, if the objective is cost minimisation, the lowest value would be preferred.

6 **Expected value** is used to differentiate between the alternatives. However, EV is a weighted average and therefore may not correspond to the actual value obtained from any specific outcome.

7 Decision points do not use probabilities. Instead, a **choice** has to be made by management between various possible alternatives. Probabilities are used at outcome points.

8 Expectations do not take into account the range of different possible outcomes and therefore the **risk** of a substantial loss. Two very different ranges of results may have the same expected value.

Now learn how to use your knowledge

Decision trees

Use your knowledge

Hints

1. A company, Trike Ltd, has the opportunity to market a new type of bicycle. Two possible courses of action are available. They can test the market or abandon the project completely. Test markets cost £150 000 and it is believed that consumer feedback is equally likely to be positive or negative.

    If the feedback is positive, Trike Ltd could market the bike or abandon the project. If the product is launched the following sales profile is forecast:

Sales	High £m	Normal £m	Low £m
Contribution	1.4	0.4	−0.25
Probability	0.3	0.6	0.10

    If test market feedback is negative, the project would be abandoned. Abandonment at any point yields £50 000 from the sale of research.

    (a) Draw a decision tree to represent the situation.

    (b) Calculate the expected values at all decision and outcome points.

    (c) Recommend a course of action on the basis of expected value.

    (d) Describe two limitations of decision tree analysis.

make use of probabilities

✓ *Answers on page 75*

Business and the economy

15 minutes

Test your knowledge

1 The manner in which the economy moves from boom to slump, in a predictable pattern over a number of years, is known as the _____ _____.

2 A boom in the economy is characterised by rapid _____ _____ above the trend rate which causes unemployment to fall.

3 Changes in the overall economy are often caused by actions taken by governments or central banks. Monetary policy actions involve the manipulation of _____ _____.

4 Recessions cause problems for businesses as customers become harder to find. However, there may be a consolation in that it becomes easier to _____ staff.

5 In recessions, the type of businesses which suffer the greatest percentage fall in sales are those that produce products or services which have a high _____ _____ _____.

6 Businesses dislike inflationary conditions because if their costs are increasing, they may have to increase their selling prices to protect _____ _____.

7 The rate of inflation is generally measured using the _____ _____ _____, which measures changes in the prices of an average consumer's shopping bill.

8 Businesses cannot escape from broader economic conditions. It is the key element of the _____ environment in which they have to operate.

Answers

7 Retail Price Index **8** external
5 income elasticity of demand **6** profit margins
1 trade cycle **2** economic growth **3** interest rates **4** recruit

 If you got them all right, skip to page 53

50

Business and the economy

30 minutes

Improve your knowledge

1. Alternatively described as the business cycle, the **trade cycle** shows economic fluctuations between boom and slump over a variable number of years. These fluctuations revolve around a general upward trend caused by technological change.

2. When **economic growth** is faster than the long-term trend of approximately 2½%, new jobs are created faster than old jobs are destroyed by technological change. Unemployment consequently decreases.

3. In the UK, monetary policy is conducted by the Monetary Policy Committee of the Bank of England. It meets once a month to set **interest rates** for the next month.

4. As personal disposable income declines in a recession, firms find it increasingly difficult to maintain sales. However, some of this economic pain may be alleviated by the fact that it is easier to **recruit** staff. The field of candidates is likely to be much wider and less remuneration is required to attract applicants.

5. Products with a high **income elasticity of demand** will suffer the greatest proportionate fall in demand as personal disposable income declines in a recession. Products with a high IED tend to be luxuries rather than necessities.

6. Rising costs exert pressure on **profit margins** unless the firm is in a strong enough position to pass on the higher costs to customers through higher prices. Whether the firm is able to do this depends upon the price elasticity of demand for their products. If this is high, an increase in selling price is likely to result in a substantial loss of customers.

7 The **Retail Price Index** is the measure of inflation used for many purposes such as updating social security benefits and by trade unions when negotiating pay rises. An alternative measure exists, known as the 'underlying' inflation rate which excludes mortgage interest from the index.

8 All businesses have to operate within an **external** environment which is largely beyond their influence. The economy is a key element of this environment.

Business and the economy

Use your knowledge

Hints

1 What is meant by the term 'cost push' inflation?

not demand pull

2 The Retail Price Index for a country, Tonga, is 334.7 in August 1998 and in September 1998 is 342.1. Calculate the percentage increase in prices over the two months.

do not just subtract the indices

3 Explain the term 'gross domestic product'.

4 Why might an increase in interest rates, implemented to reduce inflationary pressures, actually cause an increase in the RPI in the short term?

think about what the index includes

5 What is meant by 'structural unemployment'?

6 How might the policies designed to cure structural unemployment differ from those designed to correct cyclical unemployment?

different cause

7 Pilco Ltd manufactures leisure products and sells exclusively in the home market, but it does face considerable competition from imports. It has a high gearing ratio of 65% as a consequence of a substantial variable rate bank loan.

How might Pilco Ltd be affected by a sudden and significant increase in interest rates by the Monetary Policy Committee?

Answers on page 76

The international dimension

15 minutes

1 If a business decides to commence exporting a product after many years of selling it into its domestic market, there may be two additional complications to consider:

(a) a different marketing _____

(b) a different _____.

2 One way to alleviate some of the problems in 1 (a) is for a firm to employ the services of a foreign _____ who is familiar with local trading customs and practice.

3 A major problem of 1 (b) is the _____ it introduces in decisions that involve planning ahead.

4 An importer of raw materials who has purchased them on 1 August 1998, but does not have to pay for them until 31 October 1998, faces the risk of a _____ of sterling between the two dates.

5 One way the importer can remove the uncertainty is to enter into a _____ _____ _____ on 1 August 1998 which fixes the exchange rate which will be used for the conversion of 31 October 1998.

6 Exchange rates between different countries are determined, at any point in time, in the _____ _____ _____ by the forces of demand and supply.

7 If a country has a _____ exchange rate, its government is prepared to allow its external value to fluctuate every day, according to the relative demand for it.

8 Immediately after a devaluation of sterling, UK exporters can choose to reduce the price of their goods overseas or they can retain the previous price and enjoy higher _____ _____.

The international dimension

30 minutes

Improve your knowledge

1 Advertising in a foreign country can be difficult if the business is not familiar with the **culture** of that country. Advertising codes and standards vary widely between countries.

A different **currency** may be involved in the transaction, introducing an additional element of risk.

2 The use of an **agent** can minimise the risk of selling into a foreign market. An agent is a third party commissioned to undertake the selling and distribution for a particular region.

3 Conducting transactions in foreign currency introduces extra **uncertainty** into the exchange process. There is usually a time-lag in business transactions between entering into contracts and money changing hands. As currencies often fluctuate between the two dates the profitability of a contract can be significantly altered.

4 If there is a **depreciation** of sterling between 1 August 1998 and 31 October 1998, the importer will have to find more sterling to obtain any agreed amount of foreign currency. This would decrease the sterling profitability of the transaction.

5 A **forward exchange contract** is one of a variety of hedging methods that can be used to remove exchange rate uncertainty. The foreign exchange is still not collected until 31 October 1998, but the exchange rate used is the appropriate forward rate quoted on 1 August 1998.

6 The **foreign exchange market** is an international forum in which currencies are traded. Excess demand for a currency exerts upward pressure on its exchange rate whilst excess supply causes it to depreciate.

7 When a country has a **floating** exchange rate, the central bank abstains from intervention to influence its external value. The government thus takes a '*laissez-faire*' attitude towards the level of the currency.

8 An exporter, following a depreciation of its country's currency, could reduce its prices abroad to maximise penetration of that market. Alternatively, it could take a more short-term view and maintain the same price abroad but enjoy higher **profit margins**.

The international dimension

45 minutes

Use your knowledge

Hints

1 An exporter sells a product in the USA which costs £35 to manufacture in the UK (including profit). Currently the exchange rate is £1 = $1.60. If there is a 12.5% depreciation of sterling against the dollar, calculate the US price of the product in dollars, before and after the depreciation, assuming the depreciation was fully passed on to the US consumer.

multiply £s by 1.6

2 If, by contrast, the exporter maintained the original dollar price in the USA and the sterling profit margin was originally 20%, calculate the new sterling profit margin after the depreciation.

margin is a % of price

3 State three ways in which the marketing environment in a foreign country may differ from the domestic one.

4 State three ways a company may overcome these obstacles.

5 A manufacturer presently imports components from France. It believes very strongly that, over the next months, sterling is going to depreciate substantially against the franc. Suggest four ways the manufacturer can shield itself against such a movement.

hedging?

6 Explain the impact that a decision by the Monetary Policy Committee to increase interest rates may have on a company which exports half its output.

'hot money'

7 Assess the advantages and disadvantages for UK businesses of a future UK government decision to join the European single currency.

Answers on page 77

Answers to

Use your knowledge tests

Contribution and breakeven

1 (a) Variable – direct materials and direct labour.
   Fixed   – rent, rates, depreciation and insurance.

   (b) $\text{BE output} = \dfrac{\text{fixed costs}}{\text{contribution per unit}} = 125\,000 \text{ units}$

   (c) *current output*
   Profit = total revenue –   total costs
        = £60 × 150 000 – [£4 375 000 + (£25 × 150 000)]
        = £9 000 000   –   £8 125 000
        = £875 000

   full capacity output
   Profit = total revenue –   total costs
        = £60 × 200 000 – [£4 375 000 + (£25 × 200 000)]
        = £12 000 000   –   £9 375 000
        = £2 625 000

   (d) Profit   = total revenue – total costs
   £2 187 500 = P × 150 000   – £8 125 000
   £10 312 500 = 150 000P
   £68.75   = P

2 (a) Point A measures breakeven *sales revenue*. This is not the same the same as breakeven output and is measured in £s rather than units.

   (b) Distance B measures the profit at output of 30 000 units.

   (c) Distance C measures the margin of safety in units.

(d) An increase in the selling price will raise the gradient of the total revenue line. This new line will intersect with the total cost line at a lower breakeven output as shown below.

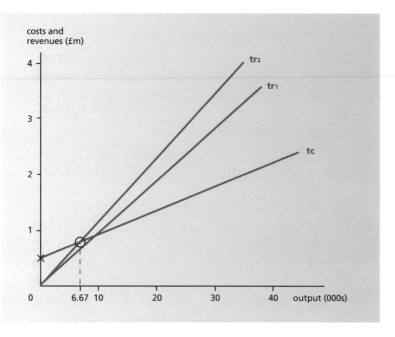

Answer = 6667 units

Balance sheets and profit and loss accounts

1 (a) **Tacky plc Balance sheet as at 30 June 1998**

	£		£
Fixed assets		*Capital and reserves*	
Land	175 000	Ordinary share capital	200 000
Buildings	100 000	Revaluation reserve	40 000
Fixtures	70 000	Retained profit	95 000
Vehicles	50 000		335 000
	395 000		
		Long term liabilities	
Current assets		Loan	150 000
Stock	25 000		
Debtors	75 000	*Current liabilities*	
Bank	50 000	Trade creditors	25 000
Cash	5 000	Tax	15 000
	155 000	Dividends	25 000
			65 000
	550 000		550 000

(b) **Tacky plc Balance sheet as at 1 July 1998**

	£	£
Fixed assets		
Land		200 000
Buildings		100 000
Fixtures		70 000
Vehicles		60 000
		430 000
Current assets		
Stock	25 000	
Debtors	75 000	
Bank	45 000	
Cash	5 000	
	150 000	

Current liabilities		
Trade creditors	25 000	
Tax	15 000	
	(40 000)	
Net current assets		110 000
		540 000
Less *Long term liabilities*		
Loan		(130 000)
		410 000
Capital and reserves		
Ordinary share capital		250 000
Revaluation reserve		65 000
Retained profit		95 000
		410 000

(c) Working capital is £110 000. If this is insufficient it may mean that the firm is unable to pay its debts which could lead to its enforced liquidation.

(d) A reserve inserted into the shareholders' funds section to maintain balance after the upward revaluation of a fixed asset such as land, buildings or investments.

(e) They generally have a finite life and therefore an asset's cost must be spread over its useful economic life.

(f) Freehold (i.e. outright ownership) land is available for an infinite number of years and there is thus no fixed life over which to spread the cost.

(g) (1) Goodwill is an intangible asset but is not generally shown on the balance sheet.

(2) Market depreciation rates may exceed those used to depreciate fixed assets in the accounts.

(3) Fixed assets such as land or buildings may not have been revalued for several years.

(h) It increases the owners' capital and therefore must be added to it on the balance sheet.

Ratio analysis

1 (a) $\text{ROCE} = \dfrac{\text{net profit before interest and tax}}{\text{capital employed}}$

$= \dfrac{113\,000}{875\,000} \times 100\% = 12.9\%$

Value is above risk free rate but may not be enough to compensate for risk present in the industry.

(b) $\text{Current ratio} = \dfrac{\text{current assets}}{\text{current liabilities}}$

$= \dfrac{£285\,000}{£185\,000}$

$= 1.54$

$\text{Acid test} = \dfrac{\text{current assets} - \text{stock}}{\text{current liabilities}}$

$= \dfrac{£285\,000 - £75\,000}{£185\,000}$

$= 1.14$

Both these ratios show a comfortable balance between liquidity and profitability.

(c) $\text{Debtors' turnover} = \dfrac{\text{debtors}}{\text{turnover}} \times 365 \text{ days}$

$= \dfrac{£190\,000}{£975\,000} \times 365 = 71 \text{ days}$

$\text{Stock turnover} = \dfrac{\text{stock}}{\text{cost of sales}} \times 365 \text{ days}$

$= \dfrac{£75\,000}{£425\,000} \times 365 \text{ days} = 64 \text{ days}$

These two ratios show that, on average, debtors take 71 days to settle their accounts and that stock resides in the business for 64 days before being sold.

(d) $\text{Gearing} = \dfrac{\text{prior charge capital}}{\text{total capital}} \times 100\%$

$$= \dfrac{£150\,000}{£875\,000} \times 100\% = 17.1\%$$

A ratio below 50% is generally considered to be low geared, so that 17.1% is significantly low. This means that the company has a fairly low exposure to the risk of interest rate changes.

(e) (1) Ordinary shareholders will see the company as a risky investment.

(2) It may be difficult to obtain future finance.

(3) Profits will fluctuate proportionately more than a low geared company.

(f) (1) A rights issue of ordinary shares.

(2) Repayment of loans out of profits.

(g) (1) Quality of management.

(2) Skills of workforce.

(3) Future demand for company's product.

(4) Industrial relations.

(h) (1) A rights issue of shares.

(2) Sale and leaseback of fixed assets.

Cash flow management

1   (a)

		£
Cash inflow		
Share capital		150 000
Bank loan		25 000
Sales		225 000
		400 000
Cash outflow		
Interest		3 750
Machinery		100 000
Raw materials		175 000
Wages		80 000
Overheads		30 000
		(388 750)
Cash balance		11 250

(b)

		£	£
Turnover			250 000
Purchases		175 000	
Closing stock		(75 000)	
Cost of sales			(100 000)
Gross profit			150 000
Less	Expenses:		
	Interest	3 750	
	Wages	80 000	
	Overheads	30 000	
	Depreciation of mach.	10 000	
			(123 750)
Net profit			26 250
Less	Appropriations:		
	Tax	6 563	
	Dividends	15 000	
			(21 563)
Profit cf			4 687

2 (1) Depreciation.

   (2) Credit sales and purchases.

   (3) Purchase or sale of fixed assets.

3 (1) To support an application for external finance.

   (2) To plan ahead for times of surplus cash.

4 (1) Negotiate new overdraft facilities.

   (2) Sale and leaseback of fixed assets.

5 Expanding too rapidly without an adequate amount of working capital.

6 Probably creditors, as they are only interested in the repayment of the debt, plus an agreed amount of interest. They do not benefit from any surpluses.

Investment appraisal

1 (a) *Ash*   £42 000 is recovered after four years.

   Therefore payback period = 4 years + $\dfrac{£8\,000}{£28\,000}$

   $$= 4.29 \text{ years}$$

   Rowan   £44 000 is recovered after three years.

   Therefore payback period = 3 years + $\dfrac{£6\,000}{£11\,500}$

   $$= 3.52 \text{ years}$$

(b) *Ash*   Average profit per year $= \dfrac{£126\,000 - £50\,000}{7}$

$= £10\,857$

Average rate of return $= \dfrac{£10\,857}{£50\,000} \times 100\%$

$= 21.7\%$

Rowan   Average profit per year $= \dfrac{£57\,000 - £50\,000}{5}$

$= £1\,400$

Average rate of return $= \dfrac{£1\,400}{£50\,000} \times 100\%$

$= 2.8\%$

(c)

Year	Discount factor
0	1
1	0.909
2	0.826
3	0.751
4	0.683
5	0.621
6	0.564
7	0.513

r = rate of discount
n = number of years into the future

(d)

Year	Discount factor	Ash DCF £	Rowan DCF £
0	1	(50 000)	(50 000)
1	0.909	7 272	7 272
2	0.826	6 608	14 868
3	0.751	6 008	13 518
4	0.683	12 294	7 855
5	0.621	17 388	932
6	0.564	15 792	–
7	0.513	14 364	–
NPV at cost of capital 10%		29 726	–5 555

(e) Ash is clearly preferable as it has the highest net present value and the largest ARR. Rowan is attractive on liquidity grounds though, as it has the shortest payback period.

(f) *Advantages*
(1) Reduces risk as it concentrates on the short term.

(2) Useful to firms with cash-flow problems.

Disadvantages
(1) It ignores the time value of money.

(2) It ignores receipts after the pay back period.

(g) They take into account the time value of money and thus discriminate in favour of projects which repay the outlay in the earlier years.

(h) (1) The level of risk associated with the project.

(2) The availability of skilled labour to run the project.

(3) Compatibility of the project with the existing corporate objectives.

(4) The reactions of pressure groups.

Targeting the market

1 A market segment is a small part of a market which has been divided up using one or more of the characteristics stated below.

2 (1) Age

(2) Sex

(3) Social class

(4) Geography

(5) Income

(6) Psychological attitudes.

3 It allows a firm to penetrate a market in greater depth and obtain a larger degree of consumer identification with the product. Mass marketing promotion is rather bland, by comparison, because it is not possible to focus on particular types of consumers.

4   *Advantages*

(1) By definition, there is no competition.

(2) As only a small segment of the market is involved, a firm can really target its marketing efforts to a concentrated audience.

Disadvantages

(1) It is risky because the firm has not diversified much and is therefore vulnerable to a collapse of its niche market.

(2) Competition is likely to follow if the firm is successful in its operations.

5   (a) E.g. SAGA type holidays for the over 50s. Emphasis on guided tours, being looked after etc. Club 18–30 holidays for a younger market with emphasis on lively Mediterranean locations.

(b) E.g. adventure type holidays for those with an outward bound lifestyle.

(c) Five star hotel accommodation for social class A etc.

Pricing strategies

1   (1) There may be few substitutes for the product and therefore a price hike causes consumers to switch to an alternative.

(2) The product may be strongly habit-forming and thus even substantial price increases do not deter many sales.

2    $$\text{PED} = \frac{\% \text{ change in quantity demanded}}{\% \text{ change in price}}$$

$$(-2) = \frac{Q}{25\%}$$

$$-50\% = Q$$

Therefore new quantity sold = 250 units per week.

New revenue = 250 × £25.00 = £6 250
Old revenue = 500 × £20.00 = £10 000

There is therefore a fall in revenue of £3 750.

This is to be expected with elastic demand |>2| as the percentage fall in demand will exceed the percentage increase in price.

3

	Tom £	Jerry £	Spike £
Direct costs (in total)	200 000	250 000	600 000
Overheads	160 000	400 000	240 000
	360 000	650 000	840 000
Total cost per unit (divide by sales)	180	130	280
Add mark-up of 25%	45	32.50	70
Selling price	225	162.50	350

4 Overheads, by their nature, are not generally related to sales as they are indirect costs. Overheads such as rent or business rates could be argued to be more of a function of how much space a product occupies in the factory rather than sales units.

If the firm uses cost-based pricing, then how overheads are allocated will affect the selling price and therefore the demand for a product.

Lean production and stock control

1 (1) Using the minimum of scarce resources.

(2) Checking quality at all stages of production.

(3) Empowering employees to check their own output.

(4) Shorter product development cycles.

2 (1) Storage.

(2) Deterioration.

(3) Interest lost on funds tied up in stock.

3 *Advantages*

(1) The system is less vulnerable to human error.

(2) Greater information is revealed, e.g. about consumer buying habits.

Disadvantages

(1) Staff will need retraining in its use.

(2) Expensive to purchase.

4 (a) 100 tons.

(b) 100 tons.

(c) ½ week.

(d) 200 tons.

(e) Zero.

5 (a) Reorder level = usage during lead time + buffer.

$$= \left(\frac{10\,000}{50} \times 2\right) + 2\,000$$

$$= 2\,400 \text{ tons}$$

(b) Number of deliveries $= \dfrac{\text{annual usage}}{\text{order size}}$

$$= \frac{10\,000}{2\,500}$$

$$= 4$$

(c) Opportunity cost = stock holding × cost per unit × interest rate

$$= 3\,250 \times £5 \times 6\%$$

$$= £975$$

Network analysis

1 (a)

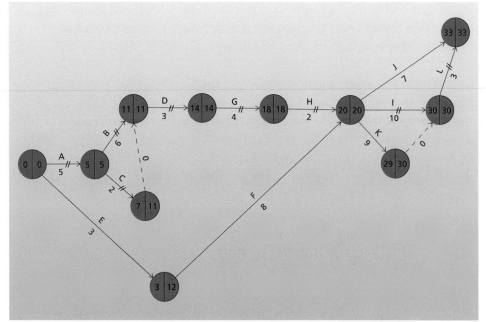

Minimum project duration is 33 weeks.

(b) Critical path is ABDGHIL.

(c)

Activity	A	B	C	D	E	F	G	H	I	J	K	L
Float	0	0	4	0	9	9	0	0	0	6	1	0

(d) Activities C, E, F, J and K all have float and could therefore be delayed up to a point without delaying the project. Length of time they can be delayed is in float table above.

(e) The just-in-time system of stock control requires that materials required for a task should arrive just as they are about to be used. The ESTs for each job can be used to pinpoint the correct arrival time for the materials to be used in that activity.

Human resource management

1   Some extent of self-management, but within clearly defined guidelines. A means by which lower level employees are allowed to exercise some discretion over the conduct of their work.

2   Most countries use an extra-employer institution to oversee training, in recognition of the fact that an individual employer may not have sufficient incentive to provide an adequate level of training. That institution could be a government agency or it could be a voluntary body set up by the whole industry. A compulsory training levy is also sometimes used where all firms have to contribute to training and there is no opt-out option.

3   $$\text{Labour turnover} = \frac{\text{number of leavers per year}}{\text{average number of staff}} \times 100$$

4   (1) Low pay.

   (2) Poor career development structure.

   (3) Authoritarian management style etc.

5   (1) Disruption to production.

   (2) Loss of experienced staff.

   (3) High retraining costs.

   (4) High recruitment costs etc.

6   A firm may have to change the typical target of their recruitment campaigns if there will be fewer young applicants. Various options are possible:

   (1) Aim more at women returners to the job market.

   (2) End age discrimination and remove maximum ages on job adverts.

   (3) Try recruitment abroad.

7 An approach to staffing where a 'core' of full-time, highly skilled, secure employees on attractive pay and conditions fulfil the essential roles within a firm.

A 'periphery' of part-time casual workers on less attractive employment conditions are used to supplement the core at busier times.

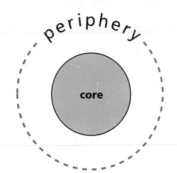

8 'Flexibility' can be seen as having a 'soft' and a 'hard' side. The soft side is not particularly controversial and uses multi-skilling and flexi-time to enjoy the benefits of an adaptable work-force. The 'hard' side involves a deterioration in workers' employment conditions such as reduced sick pay and pension rights and short-term temporary contracts.

Advantages

(1) Minimises costs.

(2) Firm is able to respond to sudden changes in demand.

Disadvantages

(1) 'Hard' side flexibility may reduce morale.

(2) Labour turnover may increase.

Work and remuneration

1 (1) There is a danger that quality of output will suffer.

(2) Output may grow at times which suit employees' need for extra money, e.g. Christmas.

2 Mayo, Maslow.

3 (1) Self-actualisation

(2) Esteem

(3) Social

(4) Safety

(5) Biological.

4   (1) Empowerment.

    (2) Consultation.

    (3) Flatter organisational structures.

5   A division of labour is a rigid demarcation of tasks where each employee
    contributes only a small repetitive part to the finished product. A high
    degree of specialisation is achieved which can increase productivity.

    The drawbacks are the impact on motivation as the endless repetition of
    small tasks can be monotonous. Also many theorists have emphasised the
    'principle of closure' whereby each worker sees a clear end product.

6   The 'Hawthorne Effect' spawned the 'human relations' school of
    management. Experiments conducted in the USA by Mayo found an
    improvement in productivity as a result of management interest in
    employees' work.

7   (1) Ignorance of the research.

    (2) Scepticism about its validity.

    (3) Costs and disruptive effects of its implementation.

8   *Advantages*

    (1) A direct link between output and remuneration.

    (2) Hard working employees will be rewarded.

    Disadvantages

    (1) It may be difficult to establish a sufficiently comprehensive
        measurement of 'performance' in this type of service industry.

    (2) May lead to certain activities being emphasised more than others.

    (3) Erodes the ethos of professionalism.

9 (1) Reduce staffing levels and use machinery instead.

(2) Reduce staffing levels and make the remaining staff work harder.

(3) Maintain staffing levels and accept lower profits.

(4) Maintain staffing levels and increase prices.

(5) Invest in training to increase the productivity of now more expensive staff.

Decision trees

1 (a)

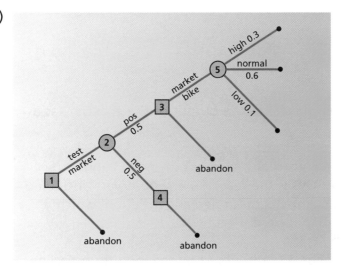

(b) *EMV 5* = (£1 400 000 × 0.3) + (£400 000 × 0.6) − (£250 000 × 0.1)
   = £635 000

EMV 4 = £50 000

EMV 3 = Greater of £50 000 or £635 000
   = £635 000

EMV 2 = (0.5 × £50 000) + (0.5 × £635 000)
   = £342 500

EMV 1 = Greater of £50 000 or [£342 500 − £150 000]

   = £192 500

(c) Using expected values, the correct decision would be to test the market, and if positive, market the bike.

(d) (1) Estimated figures are used both for the outcomes and the probabilities.

(2) Expected values are not actual specific outcomes and may cover up the small risk of a loss.

Business and the economy

1. 'Cost push' inflation is an upward pressure on prices caused by an increase in the cost of some input into production. Common examples are wages and raw materials.

2. $\% \text{ Increase} = \dfrac{342.1 - 334.7}{334.7} \times 100$

   $= 2.2\%$

3. 'Gross domestic product' is a measure of the output of the economy as a whole.

4. Mortgage interest rates are a constituent element of the RPI and therefore will cause it to rise. This is the reason many observers (including the MPC) prefer to follow movements of 'underlying inflation' which excludes mortgage interest.

5. Structural unemployment is that brought about by the long-term decline of a particular industry such as Cornish tin mines or shipbuilding.

6. The usual remedy for cyclical unemployment is some technique of demand management. However, for structural unemployment the policy needs to be more narrowly focused on an industry and/or region. Examples are retraining schemes or regional development policy.

7. Pilco Ltd will face an increase in interest costs as it is highly geared. They will also face intensified competition from imports as the higher interest rates in the UK are likely to cause a stronger pound. In addition, they may suffer from a collapse in consumer demand as leisure products have high income elasticity of demand. Disposable incomes fall as there are higher costs of servicing mortgages.

The international dimension

1   Pre-devaluation price was £35 × 1.6 = $56
    Post-devaluation price is   £35 × 1.4 = $49.

2   US price stays at $56.

    This converts into £40 sterling ($56 / 1.4).

    Cost of production is £28 (£35 × 0.8)

    New profit is therefore £12.

    $$\text{Profit margin} = \frac{\text{profit}}{\text{selling price}} \times 100$$

    $$= \frac{£12}{£40} \times 100$$

    $$= 30\%$$

3   (1) Cultural differences.

    (2) Language differences.

    (3) Political differences.

4   (1) Appoint an agent.

    (2) Set up foreign franchises.

    (3) Set up foreign production facilities.

5   (1) Purchase the francs now.

    (2) Enter into a forward exchange contract now.

    (3) Purchase the raw materials now.

    (4) Find an alternative supplier in a different country.

6   Higher interest rates in the UK will attract an inflow of 'hot money' into
    the UK which will increase the value of sterling. This gives the company
    an uncomfortable choice of either increasing their export prices or
    absorbing the change through lower profit margins.

7 Advantages

(1) Elimination of conversion costs for trade with other Euro participating countries.

(2) Removal of uncertainty about exchange rates with Euro participating countries.

(3) Greater transparency of transactions enabling an easier search for the cheapest supplier.

Disadvantages

(1) Economic policy determined by European central bank which will not be made with uniquely UK interests in mind.

(2) Competition from other Euro countries is likely to be more severe in the UK home market.